ASHFORD
TO
DOVER

including the Hythe and Sandgate branch

Vic Mitchell and Keith Smith

Cover picture details are found in caption no. 92.

Design – Deborah Goodridge

First published March 1988

ISBN 0 906520 48 7

© Middleton Press, 1988

Typeset by CitySet - Bosham 573270

Published by Middleton Press
            Easebourne Lane
            Midhurst, West Sussex
            GU29 9AZ

Printed & bound by Biddles Ltd,
            Guildford and Kings Lynn

CONTENTS

ACKNOWLEDGEMENTS

We are indebted to G. Croughton and N. Langridge for copies of tickets from their collections. We have received considerable help from many of the photographers mentioned in the captions and also from A. French, B. Hart, C.T. Orsbourne, R. Randell, A.M. Riley, E. Staff, N. Stanyon and our ever helpful wives.

Pre 1899 ownership of the main lines of Kent. (Railway Magazine)

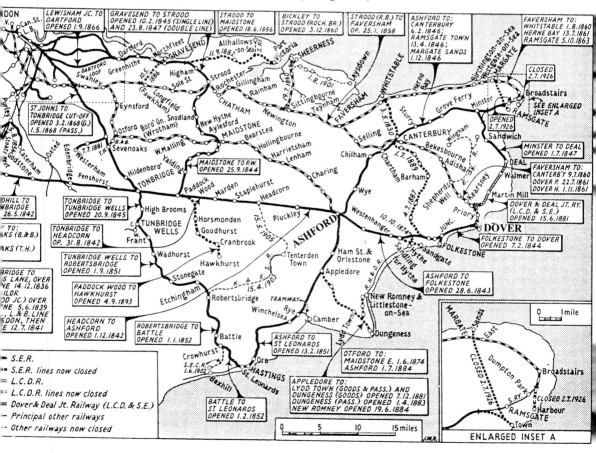

GEOGRAPHICAL SETTING

The route east from Ashford follows the upper reaches of the River Stour for about four miles, running roughly parallel to the scarp edge of the North Downs which it penetrates in Martello Tunnel, just east of Folkestone. Most of this part of the route, together with the Sandgate branch, was constructed on the well-drained sands of the Folkestone and Hythe Beds.

Between Folkestone Central and the Harbour branch junction, a viaduct carries the line over the valley formed by a narrow band of Gault Clay.

East of Martello Tunnel, the railway traverses the Warren, an unstable region of landslip, which has caused problems to generations of civil engineers. It is described in detail later in this album.

The final three miles of the seaside route, east of Folkestone, was constructed on or through the chalk exposure of the North Downs, which form part of the famed White Cliffs of Dover.

All maps are to the scale of 25″ to 1 mile, unless otherwise stated.

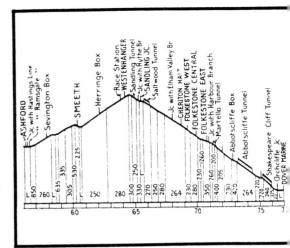

HISTORICAL BACKGROUND

The South Eastern Railway's line from London to Folkestone was the first in the area. It branched from the London & Brighton Railway at Reigate Junction (now Redhill) as Parliament under Mr. Gladstone considered that one railway to the south of the metropolis would be sufficient. It came into use on 28th June 1843, terminating at a temporary station at the west end of Folkestone's Foord Viaduct until being extended, on 18th December 1843, to a permanent station which was later to be known as Folkestone Junction or East. From here, a branch descended steeply to the harbour. Initially it only carried goods but was approved for passenger services from 1st January 1849.

The main line services were extended to Dover on 7th February 1844 but trains did not run onto the Admiralty Pier until 1861. The competing London, Chatham and Dover Railway was extended to Dover Harbour in 1861 but was not connected to the

Pier until 30th August 1864. The Pier was in fact a massive masonry breakwater, the construction of which took from 1847 until 1871.

As part of a scheme to give a more direct rail access to Folkestone Harbour, the SER opened a double track branch to Hythe and Sandgate on 9th October 1874. King Henry VIII's castle and other properties in Sandgate were purchased for demolition to allow the line to be extended east, through a lengthy tunnel, to sea level. Objections from Folkestone residents and other problems prevented the town from being thus assaulted and the sea front ruined. The branch terminus was at Seabrook, a mile west of Sandgate. The SER operated a 4-mile long standard guage street tramway between Hythe and Sandgate, it having branches inland to both Hythe and Sandgate stations. It was in use between 1891 and 1921 (apart from the war years) but plans to extend into Folkestone were also thwarted by residents who feared the import of "cheap trippers".

The Elham Valley line, which ran northwards from Cheriton Junction near Folkestone, was opened as far as Barham on 4th July 1887 and was completed through to Canterbury two years later.

Sandgate lost its train service on 1st April 1931 and passenger services ceased at Hythe during part of 1940-41 and again from May 1943 until October 1945 for military reasons. Complete closure took place on 3rd December 1951.

The Elham Valley route lost its through passenger service on 2nd December 1940, the line being taken over by the War Office. Lyminge had a limited service until May 1943 and again between October 1946 and June 1947.

An historical event was the introduction of electric traction over the entire route on 12th June 1961. Included in the scheme were the branches to Folkestone Harbour and Dover Marine, the latter station being renamed Western Docks in 1979.

SANDLING JUNCTION, HYTHE, and SANDGATE.—Southern.		

Down and *Up* week-day and Sunday timetable, dated **1924**.

E Except Saturdays.   S Saturdays only.   T 4 mins. later on Saturdays.

PASSENGER SERVICES

The initial service to Dover was of six trains on weekdays, only three of which were available to third class passengers. By 1869, there were seven return journeys, with two on Sundays. Within twenty years, the service frequency had been doubled, with additional local trains operating between Sandling Junction and Dover.

1907 saw the introduction of through trains to and from the GWR via the Redhill-Reading route and also railmotors between Dover and Sandgate. These eliminated the need for passengers to change at Sandling Junction.

The 1910 timetable showed eleven stopping and five fast trains on weekdays, with six local services on Sundays. There were several extra boat trains also.

By 1924, Folkestone Central was handling up to 20 trains daily, in both directions, with

extra on Saturdays but fewer on Sundays. By the outbreak of WWII, traffic had increased by more than 50% and the route was already a candidate for electrification.

At the height of WWII in 1942, over 20 weekday trains and 14 on Sundays were provided, mainly for service personnel.

Recovery after the war was slow, with only 23 through trains being shown on weekdays in 1948. The post-war holiday boom was in full swing ten years later, when over 30 trains traversed the route each way on Saturdays, excluding the numerous boat trains.

Following the completion of electrification in 1961 and colour light signalling in 1962, a regular interval basic service of two trains per hour was introduced. Additional services are still provided in the peak hours and for boat passengers.

ASHFORD

Ashford Station.
Boat Express.

1. The station was a terminus only briefly – between 1st December 1842 and 28th June 1843, when the line was extended to Folkestone. This Edwardian postcard features a popular photographic subject – a down boat train on the through line.
(B.C. Vigor collection)

2. A similar postcard view, but photographed from the signal gantry, shows part of the carriage sidings and goods yard. The outer platforms are only bays and did not have through lines until the station was rebuilt in 1961-62. (Lens of Sutton)

A new 10-road engine shed was opened in 1931, the year in which this 6″ to 1 mile map was published. The line to Tonbridge is on the left; to Hastings is bottom left; to Folkestone is bottom centre; to Canterbury is on the right and to Maidstone is at the top. The disused station shown close to it was the LCDR terminus, which was closed on 1st January 1899 when the SECR came into being. "Baths" were deemed noteworthy in the SER's New Town.

3. The locomotive works is largely obscured by an up boat train, in this August 1930 view from the down platform. The three groups of signals apply to trains from the bay, main and through lines, the three posts of each referring to the Canterbury, Folkestone and Hastings routes. (Lens of Sutton)

4. A typical scene from 1956 – class N1 no. 31877 blows off while taking water in the down platform as class N15 no. 30767 speeds past on the up through. In the background is D Box, which stood on a narrow spit of land between the Great Stour and East Stour rivers. (Prof. H.P. White)

5. A train of ex-GWR coaches is behind U1 class no. 31898 in this 1957 photograph. Services to the Kent coast from the Western Region were routed via Reading and Redhill. The building on the right was a refreshment room for some years. (Prof. H.P. White)

6. The up side buildings had many architectural features in common with the SER's North Camp station, which still stands today. Car parking was becoming an increasing problem when this photograph was taken in 1958 – a new station and car park followed within three years. (Prof. H.P. White)

8. Ashford E Box is on the right, close to the divergence of the line to Canterbury West. Class D1 no. 31749 accelerates past the locomotive works with 7.24 am from London Bridge, which originated at Holborn Viaduct at 6.56 am. Electrification was only three weeks away when this photograph was taken on 20th May 1961. The scheme included overhead electrification of certain sidings, such as that on the right, which led to six sorting sidings, beyond a hump. (J.J. Smith)

← ━━━━━

7. A 1960 view from the road bridge reveals that the foot bridge seen in photograph no. 1 had been removed – hence the bricked-up arch on the left. A class R1 0–4–4T is sandwiched between two vans and two horse boxes while acting as station pilot. (Prof. H.P. White)

7 | 8 | 9 | 10 | 11 | 12
SOUTHERN RAILWAY. (S.24)
(No.1) ASHFORD (KENT)
The holder is prohibited from entering
theCompanies Trains. Not transferable
Admit ONE to PLATFORM 1D
AvailableONE HOUR DAY of ISSUE ONLY
This Ticket must be given up on leaving Platform.
FOR CONDITIONS SEE BACK.
1 | 2 | 3 | 4 | 5 | 6

In 1984, the track layout was again simplified, to reduce maintenance costs and improve flexibility of operation. The speed limit through the station was increased to 85 mph. (Railway Magazine)

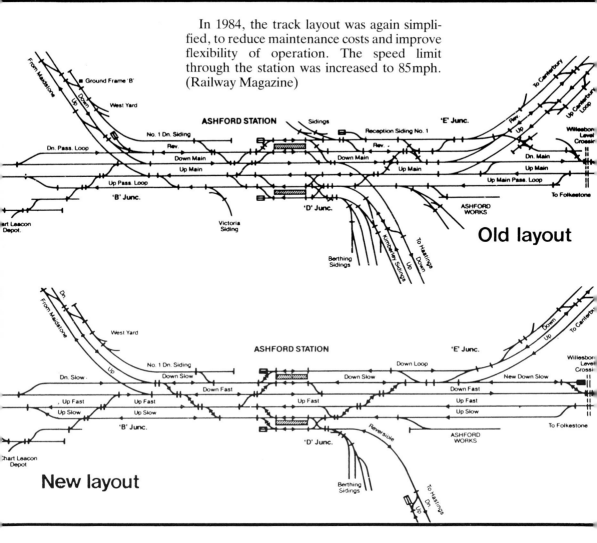

Old layout

New layout

9. With wagons of imported cars following, no. 47256 roars past on the up fast line on 22nd April 1987. On the right is the new signal box which came into use on 29th April 1962, replacing the five Ashford boxes and several more distant ones. (S.C. Nash)

Other views of this station are to be found in *Steaming through Kent* and our *Hastings to Ashford* album, which also contains a detailed map.

ASHFORD SHED

10. Opened in 1931, this shed replaced a four-road building that was attached to the works and is seen in the background of photograph no. 8. Having ceased to be a running shed, it was incorporated into the works. Note the road numbers cast indelibly into the concrete structure. A class O1 is on view, it being one of 122 built – the last one was scrapped in 1961. (S.W. Baker)

11. Also photographed in July 1946 is one of the F1 class, designed by Wainwright. The coal stage was situated on the east side of the site, the coal making the final stage of its journey, from wagon to tender, in narrow gauge steel wagons or tubs. (S.C. Nash)

The 1933 edition shows the 65ft turntable and its connection to the coal road. The line to Canterbury is at the top of the map.

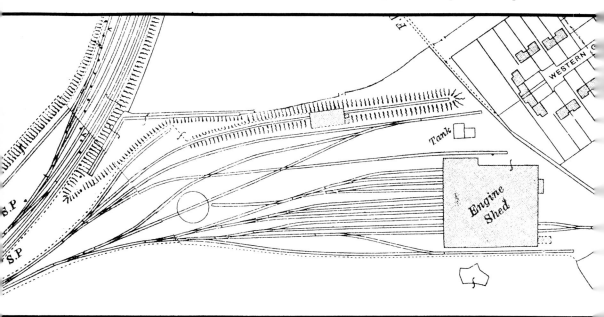

12. A 1960 photograph shows all ten roads which often accommodated over 50 locomotives. Steam ceased in 1963 but some diesel locomotives were serviced here until 1968. The water tank projects above the shed roof, on the right. (J. Scrace)

13. The Ashford Steam Centre was established after the closure of the shed and an interesting collection of rolling stock was soon gathered. Lined up on 26th October 1969 are H class no. 263, O1 class no. 65 and C class no. 592. After prolonged difficulties, the exhibits were dispersed (nos. 263 and 592 to the Bluebell Railway) and the shed demolished. (S.C. Nash)

ASHFORD WORKS

14. The works entrance was an unusual subject for a postcard sent as a birthday card to a girl in Tonbridge in 1907! The clock tower features in many photographs of the area and is now a listed structure.
(D. Cullum collection)

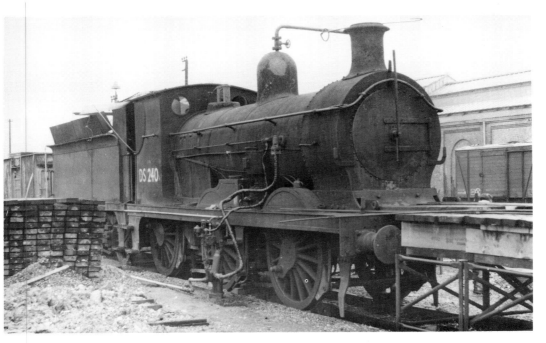

16. Steam for the works was supplied in October 1966 by C class no. DS240, formerly no. 31271. At this time the works was only producing components. A steam powered feed water pump stands in front of the centre driving wheel. (S.C. Nash)

15. The locomotive works were in use from 1847 until 1962, part of the premises still being in use in 1988 for the maintenance of rail-mounted cranes. A general view of the erecting shop on 21st May 1939 shows two overhead cranes. (S.W. Baker)

LEAVING ASHFORD

17. West of the Hastings line, a fan of eleven sidings spread out to serve Ashford Wagon Works. This is the scene on 8th October 1966 as C class no. DS239 (formerly no. 31592) works the yard, with an unusually crowded footplate. After surviving on export orders for some time, the works closed down in 1981. (S.C. Nash)

18. With collector shoes down, electro-diesel no. 73147 hums past the site of the sorting sidings and locomotive shed, on 6th June 1983. The train is the 12.21 Speedlink service from Paddock Wood to Dover, and is approaching Willesborough Crossing, which was then still manually operated. (J.S. Petley)

19. The splitting signal for the up slow line is on the left as no. 73146 speeds south on 5th June 1982, with the then recently introduced British portion of the "Venice Simplon Orient Express". In the background are the railway yard lighting towers and the footbridge adjacent to Willesborough Crossing. This was the only public vehicular level crossing on the SER main line between Reigate Junction and Dover Town and remains so today. Two new sidings are planned in this vicinity for the transfer of Channel Tunnel spoil from rail to road. (J.S. Petley)

20. Sevington Signal Box was 1½ miles from Ashford and was closed when the panel box opened on 29th April 1962. Class N 2–6–0 no. 31810 climbs at 1 in 260, with a down freight on 20th May 1961. (J.J. Smith)

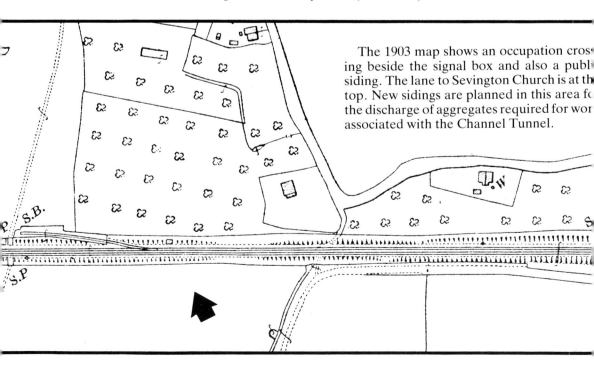

The 1903 map shows an occupation crossing beside the signal box and also a public siding. The lane to Sevington Church is at the top. New sidings are planned in this area for the discharge of aggregates required for work associated with the Channel Tunnel.

21. The station was opened in October 1852 and served a scattered community which still numbers under 1000 persons. This view is of the up side and includes a double armed signal post. (Lens of Sutton)

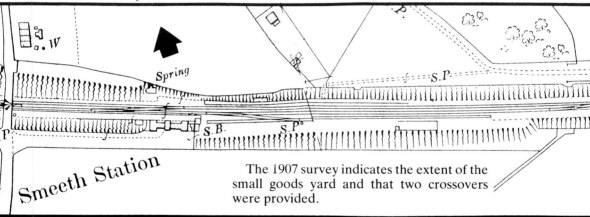

Smeeth Station

The 1907 survey indicates the extent of the small goods yard and that two crossovers were provided.

22. The usual SER staggered platforms and weather-boarded signal box were provided. The road bridge now carries the B2069 to Smeeth Church, which is ¾ mile to the north. (Lens of Sutton)

23. The down platform had the minimum of facilities as most originating traffic was for Ashford or London. The lanterns contained paraffin lamps, the posts being of the twisted barley-sugar type. (Lens of Sutton)

24. Unusual on the SER was the multi-gabled building. The nearest gable and the wooden structure were later additions. Passenger services were withdrawn on 4th January 1954 but goods facilities lasted until 18th April 1964. (Lens of Sutton)

25. Photographed on 20th May 1961, the signal box then had limited life, being closed on 29th April 1962. The goods yard is partly fenced and was let for commercial use after its closure on 18th April 1964. All the buildings were later razed. (J.J. Smith)

26. Herringe Box was half way between Smeeth and Westenhanger and was a block post opened only at busy times. All signals are off as the Victoria to Folkestone Harbour boat train passes by on 20th May 1961. Two sidings, on the up side, were laid in WWII for rail-mounted guns. They were named after the nearby village of Sellindge. (J.J. Smith)

WESTENHANGER

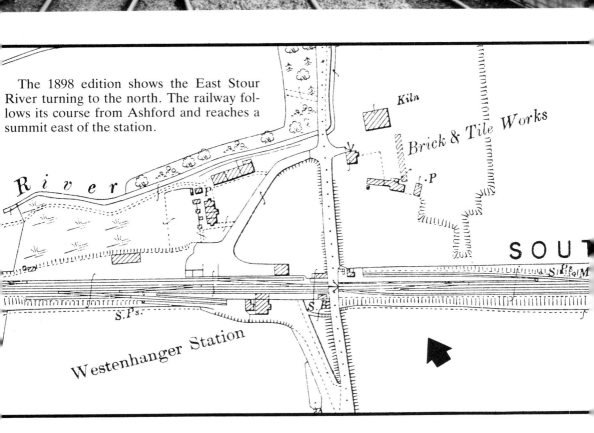

The 1898 edition shows the East Stour River turning to the north. The railway follows its course from Ashford and reaches a summit east of the station.

Kiln

Brick & Tile Works

River

P

P

SOUT

S.Ps.

S.E

S.P. & M

Westenhanger Station

27. Initially the only intermediate stopping place between Ashford and Folkestone, the station was "Westenhanger and Hythe" until October 1874, when the Sandgate branch opened and it became the junction station. An 1879 photograph shows the first signal box on the left and its replacement opposite it. (Lens of Sutton)

28. Coaching stock is seen berthed on both sides of this picture and a train stands in the bay platform beyond the bridge. The nearby Folkestone Racecourse generated additional traffic, not only in passengers but in horse-boxes also. The third signal box is visible. (Lens of Sutton)

SOUTHERN RAILWAY.
ONE DOG AT OWNER'S RISK
(accompanied by Passenger)
Westenhanger to
3D. any Station on the
SOUTHERN RAILWAY
not exceeding 10 miles.
This Ticket is available for one journey only and must be given up at destination Station
FOR CONDITIONS SEE BACK
0049   0049

29. A down train arrives behind class L no. 765 in about 1920, having passed by the four racecourse platforms, visible in the distance. They are now disused but additional stops are made by scheduled services at the main platforms on race days.
(S.C. Nash collection)

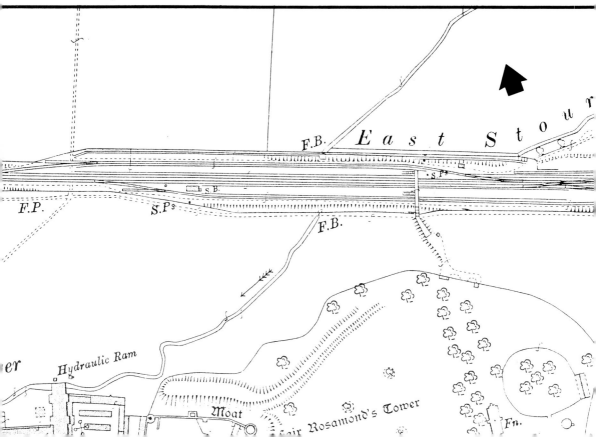

F.B.   *East Stour*

F.B.

F.P.   S.P.

Hydraulic Ram

Moat   Fair Rosamond's Tower   Fn.

30. The building was erected in 1861 to replace the original timber structure. Only a few trains now call in the peak hours and the station is only staffed on race days. A note on earlier transport history: the road over the bridge is of Roman origin, being Stone Street, which linked Canterbury and Lympne. (Prof. H.P. White)

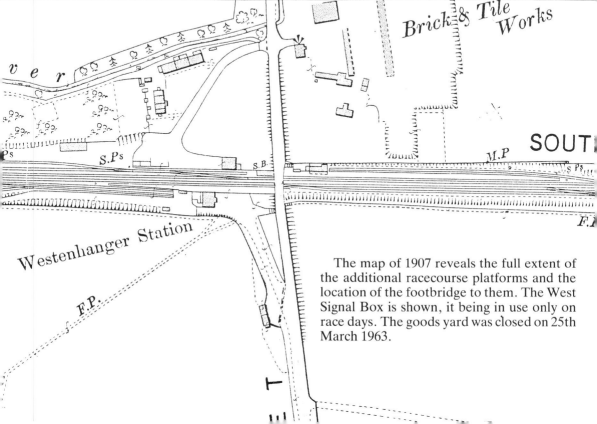

The map of 1907 reveals the full extent of the additional racecourse platforms and the location of the footbridge to them. The West Signal Box is shown, it being in use only on race days. The goods yard was closed on 25th March 1963.

SANDLING

The 1907 edition shows the lavish double track arrangements provided for the branch. Had it reached Folkestone as planned, this layout would have been justified.

31. Opened as Sandling Junction on 1 January 1888, more than 13 years after th branch came into use, it lost its suffix whe the Hythe line was closed in December 195 The branch is on the right of this 1891 view which shows the footbridge in the process o receiving a roof.(Lens of Sutton)

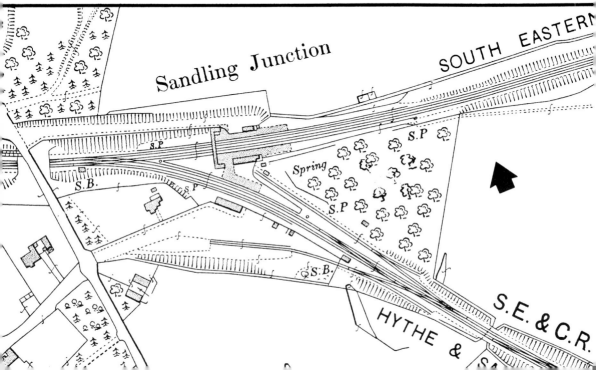

32. The branch was singled in 1931 and it is doubtful if the up branch platform was ever used. Its site is shown as a grass bank in this 1957 view. The booking office thus remained remote from the platforms, access to them being via the foot crossing in the distance. (A.E. Bennett)

33. The exterior, in 1957, showed its similarity of design to Nutfield station. At this time a number of camping coaches were located in this delightful rural environment. Several retired Pullman cars served this purpose until 1967. (A.E. Bennett)

34. Another 1957 picture shows the former up line on the left, retained as a goods loop, and the truncated single line to Hythe on the right, used then as a headshunt. (A.E. Bennett)

35. Battle of Britain class no. 34089 *602 Squadron* passes the former no. 1 Box and the branch catch points on 20th July 1957. This box became obsolete on 18th February 1962 with the introduction of colour light signals between Smeeth and Archcliffe Junction. No. 2 Box can be seen in the background of the 1891 photograph. (A.E. Bennett)

SOUTHERN RAILWAY.
H. M. FORCES ON LEAVE.
Available for Three Days including Day of issue

0170

Shorncliffe to

Shorncliffe
Canterbury West

Shorncliffe
Canterbury West

0170

CANTERBURY WEST
Via Ashford or Elham

THIRD CLASS   THIRD CLASS

FOR CONDITIONS SEE BACK

36. A 1958 view includes the lengthy canopy on the down platform which has more recently been replaced by a small glazed shelter. Access to the platforms is via the ramp near the up starting signal. (H.C. Casserley)

37. An August 1987 photograph is included to show an example of the rolling stock introduced for the Kent Coast electrification. Most units were extensively refurbished in 1980-83. The footbridge has lost its roof but the up platform retains at least part of its canopy. (J. Scrace)

38. The original entrance building, seen in picture no. 33, has been demolished, its site now being part of the car park. The booking office is now situated in the former up waiting room, the south elevation of which is seen here. (J. Scrace)

HYTHE &
SANDGATE BRANCH

39. Nearly ½ mile south-east of Sandling Junction the branch passed through the 94 yard long Hayne Wood Tunnel. The 2.55 pm from Hythe is seen after emerging from it on 13th May 1950, hauled by H class no. 31520. In the foreground is the goods loop seen earlier. (S.C. Nash)

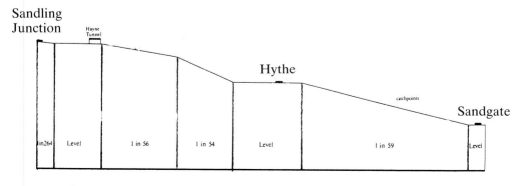

Sandling
Junction

Hayne
Tunnel

Hythe

catchpoints

Sandgate

1 in 264 | Level | 1 in 56 | 1 in 54 | Level | 1 in 59 | Level

HYTHE

40. Looking towards the 1 in 54 gradient up to Sandling Junction in 1921, we can marvel at the extent of the down platform canopy. Milepost 67 partly obscures the second house provided for the station master. Gas lighting was installed here and at the adjacent two stations in 1910. (S.C. Nash collection)

The 1898 map indicates that there were approach roads to both sides of the station. The house at the end of the southern one was the first station master's dwelling. The tracks of the street tramway are seen to connect with a siding in the goods yard.

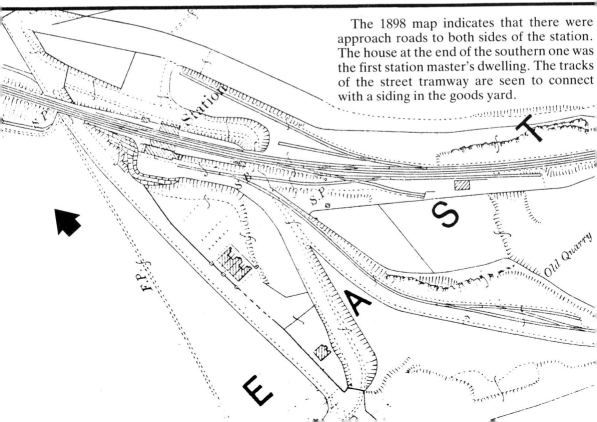

41. The buildings nearest to the signal box in this 1950 photograph are the gentlemen's toilet and the station master's office. These were added in 1899, the original gents at the other end of the main building being converted to a parcels office, which was later destroyed by a bomb in WWII. (D. Cullum)

42. A C class is seen at the head of the last train from Hythe – the 4.20 pm on 1st December 1951. The signal box had been closed 20 years earlier and the down platform had been shortened, as it was only used for parcels. The SR added the suffix "Kent" to the name in 1925 and in 1931 it was changed to "Hythe for Sandling". It remained so until WWII. (S.C. Nash)

SANDGATE

43. An eastward view from 1891 shows the engine shed and water tank in the distance. Had the line been extended to Folkestone Harbour as planned, this station would have been renamed Seabrook and a new one built closer to Sandgate. (Lens of Sutton)

44. The eastern end of the Royal Military Canal is seen between the coast and the station. Also visible is the 17-lever signal box and the route of the railway up the 1 in 59 gradient to Hythe. Until the track was rearranged in 1900, trains arrived at the shelterless down platform. A departing train is illustrated in this early postcard.
(S.C. Nash collection)

45. In its final years the building on the down platform was used as a goods shed and is seen in 1921, propped up and with boards missing. The obverse of the board on the left bore the word GENTLEMEN. The building survived the station by many years, being retained for the comfort of East Kent bus crews. Both it and the bus garage have been superseded by houses. (S.C. Nash collection)

The land to the north of the station was shown as War Department property, on this 1898 edition. The highway crossing it was the Military Road which led to the massive Shorncliffe Camp. The sea front tramway and its connection to the railway is also evident. This was sometimes used for the conveyance of building materials, particularly for repairing the sea wall, and was operated briefly by a small locomotive.

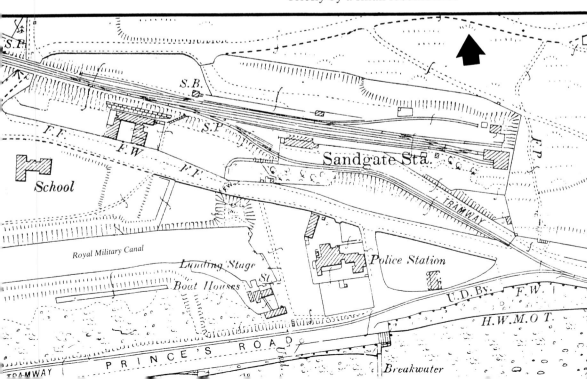

46. The Folkestone, Sandgate and Hythe Tramway was operated by the SER using horses. Plans to electrify the route and complete it to Folkestone in 1907 were opposed by the objectors of that town, who deemed that the overhead wires would be unsightly. The SER also built and operated the Imperial Hotel at Seabrook, the trams stopping at the door. Car no. 1 is seen at the eastern terminus by the Royal Oak at Sandgate. Nos. 2 and 4 were of similar design; no. 5 was an open "toast rack" and no. 3 was fully glazed, for use in winter. (S.C. Nash collection)

CHERITON JUNCTION

47. Looking towards Folkestone on 18th July 1953, we see a train loaded with steel sleepers, lifted from the Elham Valley line which had closed to passengers six years earlier. A third track, known as the down local, ran from here to Shorncliffe and can be seen in front of the signal box. The fresh ballast is on the site of the then recently removed up connection. (J.J. Smith)

CHERITON HALT

48. Part of the halt is visible in this interesting photograph from about 1913. It had a chequered history being in use from 1st May 1908 to 1st December 1915 and from 14th June 1920 to 1st February 1941. It was also open between 7th October 1946 and 16th June 1947, during the partial reopening of the Elham Valley route. (Lens of Sutton)

49. Type 2 class 24 no. D5010 approaches the junction with a bank holiday relief train from Dover Priory to London Bridge on 22nd May 1961. An additional up track was laid as far as the junction, giving quadruple track to Folkestone Central. Cheriton may soon become a household word, associated with the start of family holidays at the Channel Tunnel Terminal, to be built nearby. (S.C. Nash)

FOLKESTONE WEST

50. Opened as Shorncliffe Camp on 1st November 1863, the suffix Camp was dropped in 1926. A new enlarged station was opened on 1st February 1881 and the road bridge removed. This small wooden building, photographed in 1871, was retained as a goods shed and office and is marked in black on both maps. (Lens of Sutton)

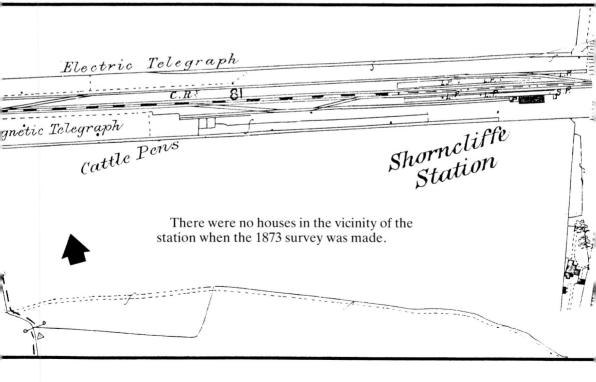

There were no houses in the vicinity of the station when the 1873 survey was made.

51. The new spacious station included quadruple track between the platforms and every
comfort for passengers – note the eight chimney stacks on the up side. The white patches
on the cattle wagons are due to the use of a
limewash antiseptic. Admire the styling of
the gas lamp. (P. Rutherford)

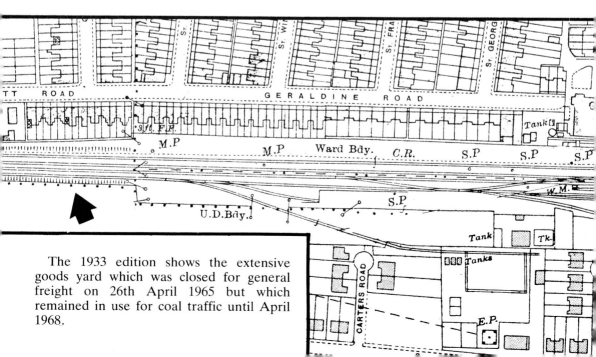

The 1933 edition shows the extensive
goods yard which was closed for general
freight on 26th April 1965 but which
remained in use for coal traffic until April
1968.

52. Ex-LSWR class L12 no. 433 accelerates on the up through, as the porter and goods guard check that all is in order. The bend in the platform edge in the foreground was eliminated when the quadrupling was extended in 1961. (H.C. Casserley)

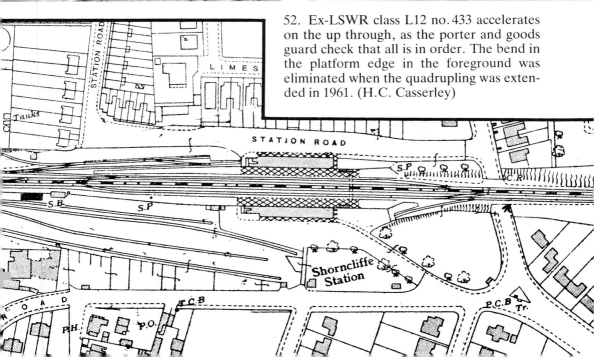

53. Schools class no. 30923 *Bradfield* is more
than half way up the continuous climb from
Dover to Sandling Tunnel when photographed on 4th September 1950. By 1987, the
up side had only two chimneys left and the
down side had four. (D. Cullum)

54. De-icing unit no. 011, formed from a
4SUB unit, runs towards Folkestone Central
on a bright November afternoon in 1986. The
Kent climate in winter has often kept these
units fully occupied. The station name was
changed to Folkestone West on 10th September 1962. (J. Scrace)

55. Unusually, the buildings on both platforms are almost identical. This is the up side. The SER offered every luxury at their new station in an attempt to entice passengers away from their other station in Folkestone. An agreement with the rival LCDR stated that receipts from Dover and Folkestone should be pooled and shared equally. But it did not mention *Shorncliffe!*. Subsequent litigation cost the SER dearly. (J. Scrace)

FOLKESTONE CENTRAL

56. The temporary terminus was sited here in 1843 but it was not until 1st September 1884 that a permanent station was opened. Known initially as "Cheriton Arch", it became "Radnor Park" two years later and finally "Folkestone Central" on 1st June 1895. The covered footways at the east end are seen during reconstruction work in May 1890. (Lens of Sutton)

The 1907 survey reveals the length of the up bay platform and the cramped nature of the approach road.

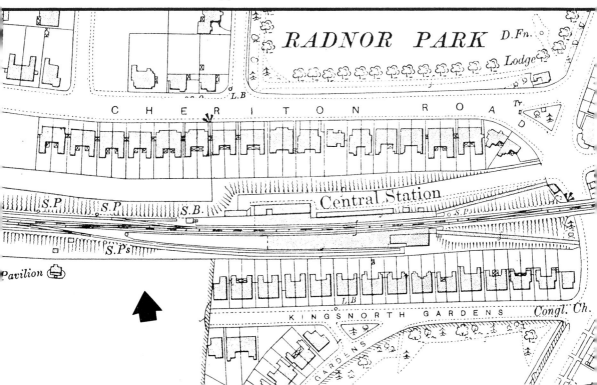

57. A postcard from about 1920 shows the unimpressive effect that this "after-thought" station had on the locality. The main entrance was, and is, tucked into a side road on the north side. (Lens of Sutton)

58. Coaches commonly stood in the up bay awaiting attachment to London bound trains. The "Man of Kent" was regularly strengthened in this manner. Most SER signal boxes were fitted with sash windows and kept cleaner than this one. (P. Rutherford)

59. A class L pauses on its circuitous journey with the 1.50 pm Margate to Maidstone East service on 11th August 1949. The exposed windswept position of the platforms is evident here. (S.C. Nash)

60. The station was totally rebuilt in 1960-61, to give two island platforms and quadruple track west to Cheriton Junction. Nos. 73220 and 73136 return empty wagons to Betteshanger Colliery on 2nd June 1983 for refilling with waste materials which were being used for the construction of new embankments near Norwood Junction. (J.S. Petley)

61. The reintroduction of inter-regional services has given the town direct access to many Midland and Northern towns. The 7.49 Liverpool to Dover service stops behind no. 47556 on 24th April 1987, while EMU no. 1583 stands behind the luggage lift. (S.C. Nash)

62. The graceful 19-arch Foord Viaduct takes the line across the deep valley and gives passengers their first sight of the harbour. Photographed in 1923, the arches, which are up to 100ft high, have subsequently been fitted with steel tie rods. (D. Cullum collection)

FOLKESTONE EAST

Opened as Folkstone in 1844, the middle "e" was added
in 1849 and "Junction" in 1852. "Shorncliffe" was added
until 1863, and from 1884 until 1897 the name reverted to
plain "Folkestone", after which "Junction" was added
again! The final change was on 10th September 1962,
when it became Folkestone East for its final three years.

63. An eastward view in about 1895 includes
the then customary low, short, staggered
platforms and fully ballasted track. Although
looking tidy, the practice was soon banned as
rotten sleepers could remain undetected.
(S.C. Nash collection)

Interesting features on the 1873 edition
include facilities for coke production (early
locomotives did not use coal) and a carriage
shed that would have required a great deal of
shunting by man power or with a horse. The
harbour branch is at the bottom of the map.

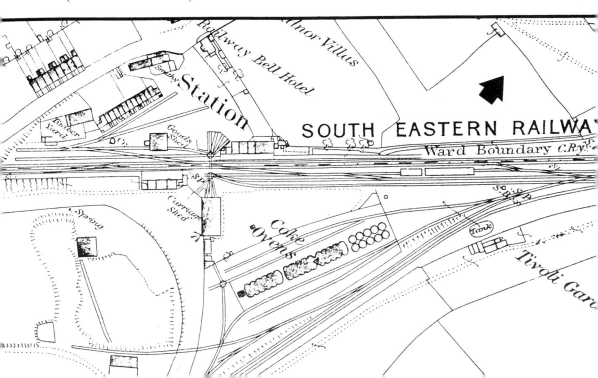

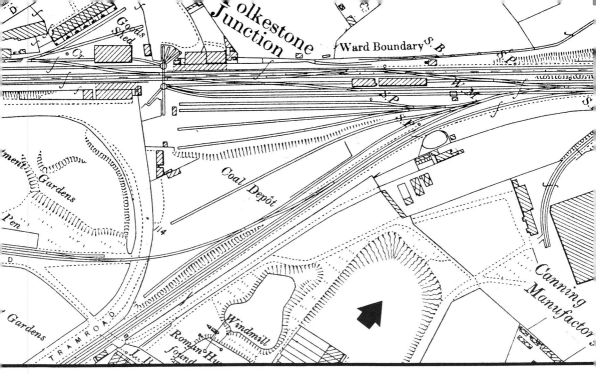

64. An F class 4–4–0 speeds west, past the small engine shed. The early maps shows two sheds, end to end. The down starting signal has a white dot instead of a stripe – other examples of this SER practice are to be found in our *Reading to Guildford* album. (S.C. Nash collection)

The 1898 edition shows the transition of the junction as a railway centre. The gardens have given way to a factory and separate areas are provided for coal and cattle.

65. The small signal box in the previous picture was replaced by this massive structure as traffic increased. Class L1 no. A753 is signalled for Dover, on 14th May 1927. The SR used the prefix A for ex-SECR engines (A meaning built at Ashford), replaced by the numeral 1 in 1931. (H.C. Casserley)

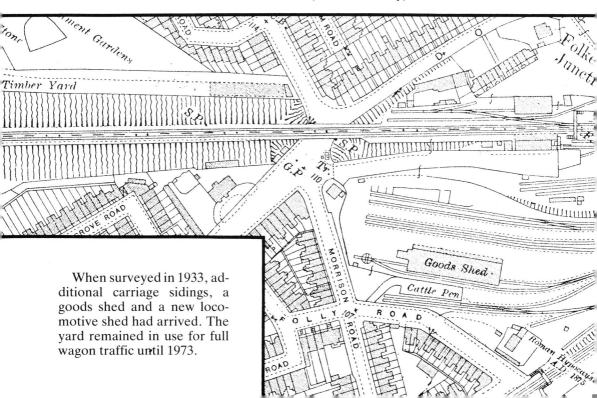

When surveyed in 1933, additional carriage sidings, a goods shed and a new locomotive shed had arrived. The yard remained in use for full wagon traffic until 1973.

66. The up side changed little over the years; neither did the small goods yard on the right. This was the first main line to be seen by visitors to Britain via Folkestone! Until 1930, a second signal box, Folkestone Junction B, was in use and was located on the east side of Martello Tunnel. (Lens of Sutton)

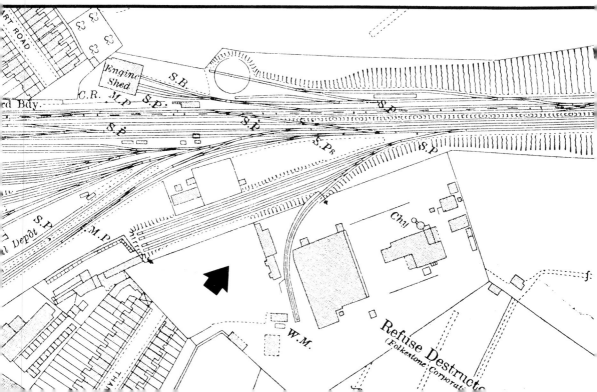

67. Looking east, we see straight through the 532 yd long Martello Tunnel, which was named after the tower above it. On the left is the end of the North Downs and a Britannia

class locomotive being prepared outside the shed for the next up "Golden Arrow". The down service used Folkestone regularly in the 1952-60 period. (Lens of Sutton)

68. A close-up of the unique brake van, seen on the right of the previous picture, shows that it was built on the chassis of a former six-wheeled tender. The braking of loose coupled goods trains on the 1 in 30 gradient down to the harbour was an exceptional problem. This vehicle carried a large number of concrete weights and also sanding equipment – the discharge pipes are evident. (P. Hay)

69. All trains to and from the harbour had to reverse in one of three sidings that terminated near the mouth of Martello Tunnel. Up to four tank engines would handle the train on the branch. Here no. 34075 *264 Squadron* has been attached to take the train on to Victoria on 21st May 1956. (E. Wilmshurst)

70. A three-road engine shed, with integral water tank, was erected at the end of WWI. Accommodation was for six locomotives and a 65ft turntable was provided. Two of the allocation are seen in store on 24th March 1957, with covers on their chimneys. (D. Clayton)

72. The 4.25 am special train from Fishguard Harbour enters the sidings on 14th June 1958. It carried handicapped people who were believed to be travelling from Ireland to Lourdes in search of a cure – great was the diversity of railway traffic. Class S15 no. 30835 had hauled the train from Redhill – this class was a very unusual sight on the Eastern Section after WWII. Class R1 no. 31337 can be seen with a lid on its chimney and a trio of R1s wait to work down the branch. (J.J. Smith)

71. Another 1957 photograph shows an up boat train snaking out of the middle siding (No. 1 Train Road) behind 1926-built class N15 no. 30798, while a down service waits in the platform. Second class is shown on the doors. This class had been abandoned in 1915 except on boat trains – 1st and 3rd being the usual options in 1957. (Prof. H.P. White)

73. Major earthworks were undertaken before three additional sidings could be provided for the berthing of 12-coach electric trains. The three original sidings are in the centre of this February 1960 photograph, and were soon to be electrified. (British Rail)

The 6″ to 1 mile map shows the extent of
the harbour sidings in 1931. Goods traffic
ceased on 17th August 1968.

FOLKESTONE HARBOUR BRANCH

74. Half of the mile long branch is at the severe gradient of 1 in 30. Two class R1 0–6–0Ts haul up the empty stock of the "Golden Arrow" on 12th May 1956, while another one banks at the rear. No. 31339 leads – it was one of those cut down to fit the small tunnel on the Whitstable branch. East Cliff level crossing is now used by pedestrians only. (S.C. Nash)

75. The R1s were replaced by ex-GWR pannier tanks in 1959. A pair are seen struggling up the incline, parallel to the highway still known as The Tram Road. Folly Road crossing is now protected by lifting barriers and the concrete footbridge, from which this photograph was taken in 1959, has been retained. (Prof. H.P. White)

76. On reaching the shore, the line passed a signal box and crossed the harbour on a series of brick arches and swing bridge, the end of which can be seen on the right. Class R1 no. A338 is banking an up train on 31st March 1929. The incline commences half way across, as evidenced by the arch heights. (H.C. Casserley)

78. Three full height R1s storm across the viaduct at 1.40 pm on 18th October 1958. This classical view across the inner harbour shows the present steel bridge span and a strengthened arch. (S.C. Nash)

77. The first swing bridge was erected in 1847, the viaduct serving as the railway pier for four years prior to this. The bridge was rebuilt in 1893 and again in 1930. Here we see class R1 no. A153 crossing it on 14th May 1927, with a cut down cab and full length chimney! (H.C. Casserley)

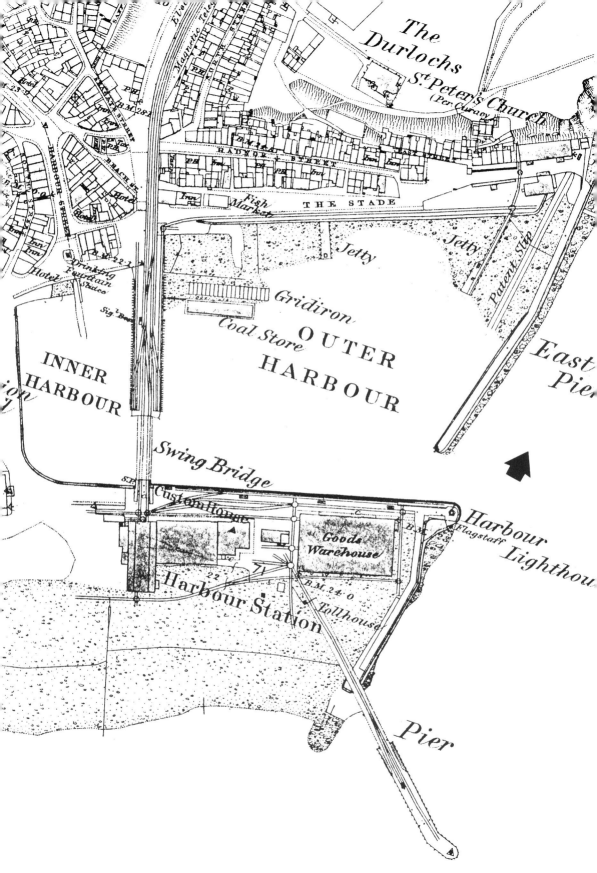

FOLKESTONE HARBOUR

79. Platforms 1 and 2 were built on the site of the original terminal station, numbers 3, 4 and "Lighthouse" being on the pier. Trains were running to a platform on the pier by 1883 but local residents preferred to entrain at the harbour station to avoid climbing the hill. (Lens of Sutton)

The 1881 edition shows quadruple track on the original SER pier and the company's rail connected works on the right. (The buildings were sold to the Corporation in 1928). The Harbour station came into use on 1st January 1849, when passenger services commenced on the branch. The station was built on a natural spit of shingle which formed the harbour. This the SER had acquired in semi-derelict condition in 1843. The spit was widened by the simple measure of extending a stone groyne steadily southwards from the lighthouse to "catch" the eastward drifting shingle. From the spit, the SER started building the New Pier out to sea, from which their ferries could sail regardless of tide height.

80. A 1924 photograph shows the point of commencement of the incline; details of the second swing bridge; concrete and wooden signal posts, and a fine pair of SER water columns with their characteristic large wheel controls. (Pamlin Prints)

81. A footbridge over the goods line was provided between platforms 2 and 3. Only the two platforms seen in this 1921 view now remain, much lengthened. A wall has been built on the site of the bridge. (P. Rutherford)

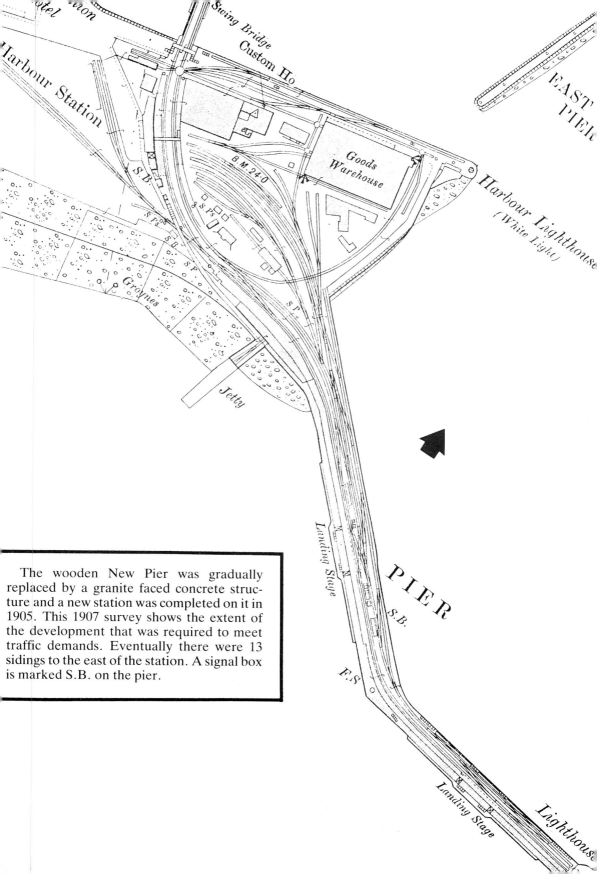

Swing Bridge

Custom Ho

Harbour Station

EAST PIER

Harbour Lighthouse
(White Light)

Goods Warehouse

B.M. 24·0

S.B.

S.B.

S.B.

S.P.

S.P.

S.P.

Groynes

Jetty

Landing Stage

PIER

S.B.

F.S.

The wooden New Pier was gradually replaced by a granite faced concrete structure and a new station was completed on it in 1905. This 1907 survey shows the extent of the development that was required to meet traffic demands. Eventually there were 13 sidings to the east of the station. A signal box is marked S.B. on the pier.

Landing Stage

Lighthouse

82. The footbridge gave access to the pier which was subject to a toll, the ticket office being more obvious in the previous photograph. The reverse curves of the track reflect the history of the site and emphasise the lack of foresight in the choice of the position of the pier. (D. Cullum collection)

83. The loco crews relax as they wait for passengers to disembark on 17th September 1955. The signal box in the distance was still in use in 1988 and controlled lifting barriers at the adjacent level crossing. (J.H. Aston)

84. One of the faithful R1s is seen with a Stephenson Locomotive Society's special in platform 3 on 19th May 1957. Owing to the limited visibility on the platform, banner repeater signals were fitted under the canopy. Limited clearances prevented the use of main line locomotives and Z class 0–8–0Ts, which were tried in 1950 and 1952 respectively. (S.C. Nash)

85. A final look at the harbour shows the S-shape station which was substantially rebuilt in 1938-39 and refurbished in 1980. The coastal freighter on the left is moored where SER steamers berthed prior to the construction of New Pier. The berth was confusingly known as South Pier. (Lens of Sutton)

Alongside the train are Mr. Newburn (director), Hon. James Byng (director), Sir Edward Watkin (chairman, with extra long coat), Mr. John Shaw (secretary), Mr. Charles Sheath (clerk to the chairman) and the guard is Mr. George Privett, who later became one of the SER's first two district superintendents.

86. The first serious landslip in The Warren occurred in 1877, closing the line for three months and destroying over 100 yards of the Martello Tunnel. The official reopening is witnessed here, the train comprising two brake vans, in which there were no seats (the guard was expected to stand in the observatory for the whole journey) and a first class three-compartment coach, hauled by an E class Cudworth 2–4–0. Note the low dog compartment, nearest the camera.
(D. Cullum collection)

87. The second major slip took place on the moonlit evening of 19th December 1915. The railway watchman was able to stop the 6.10pm Ashford to Dover train as it emerge from Martello Tunnel, hauled by D clas no. 493. No derailment took place at the tim but this was the scene next morning, afte further slippage had taken place. The lin was closed until August 1919, adding greatl to the difficulty of moving to and from Dove in WWI. (Lens of Sutton)

88. In 1888 a halt was opened to bring visitors to this unique landscape to enjoy the unusual ecology. A footbridge was built in 1889 but approval for the halt had not been sought from the Board of Trade. On discovering an unauthorised station, they refused consent. It was not officially opened until 1st June 1908, after which the tea room, seen on the cliff, was opened. (Lens of Sutton)

89. The footbridge was built from old double-head running rails and was of similar construction to the one still in use at Wokingham. Another postcard shows that it was a popular location in summer. Closure took place on 25th September 1939.
(Lens of Sutton)

The instability of the area is due to a thick layer of porous chalk lying on a thin (150ft) bed of impervious, potentially unstable gault clay, which in turn rests on a stable bed of lower greensand. All the strata dip slightly inland, north-eastwards.

With the development of the science of soil mechanics prior to WWII, it was realised that the problems were not due to the sea simply eroding the clay and its apparent slippery nature.

Borings revealed that the weight of the chalk increased enormously after prolonged rainfall, as its water table rose. It was also discovered that the slips had occurred in an arc, similar to that taken by a baby in an over-soaped bath. It was also revealed that the clay had good shear strength, except after movement in wet conditions.

Nature, as if sensitive to the pressures of world wars, contrived another slip which closed the railway completely for six weeks from November 1939 until January 1940 and partially for some months thereafter.

Serious preventive measures started in 1948, involving:

a) The boring of 14 near horizontal drainage tunnels into the chalk cliff face, to reduce the weight of water carried in the ground.

b) Toe weighting. This was equivalent to applying pressure to the ankles of the soapy baby.

c) Protecting the clay outcrop from sea erosion. Only this measure had been tried previously.

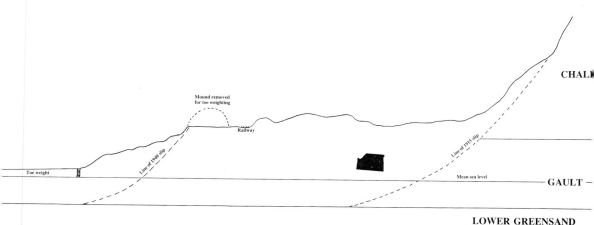

90. Toe weighting is seen as extremely worthwhile. The 1948 work is the rectangular area nearest the camera, the tapered part being added in 1951-52. The outer walls comprise 2¼-ton concrete blocks, cast on site and joined with old rails. Rock from Meldon Quarry was brought from Devon and hand packed as a base layer. Onto this, a weight of some 43,000 tons of chalk was placed. Warren Halt was retained for use by staff, its replacement being visible at the top of the picture. The white plant workshops contrast with the black ash roadways. Natural forces were in action again on 16th October 1987, when the hurricane force winds that devastated south-east England forced the *M.V. Hengist* ashore on the concrete apron. (British Rail)

The headings, for water drainage, pass ⟶
under the railway and have been surveyed
regularly to detect ground movement.
(Railway Magazine)

91. The second picture, taken in 1953, shows the length of earlier sea wall which was widened and weighted in the following two years. Left of centre is the concrete mixer, used for producing the blocks and protective covering over the chalk weighting. Above centre, there is evidence of chalk removal, this area being used as the source of much of the weighting material. The unusual problems and their costly remedies must make this one of the most expensive mile of railway in Britain (British Railway)

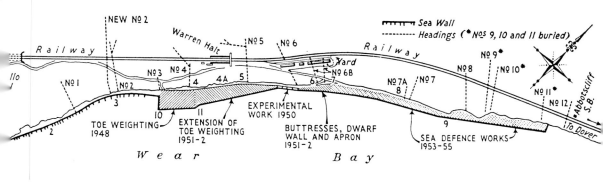

92. The jib of a crane is seen above Britannia class no. 70004 *William Shakespeare*, as it heads the all Pullman up "Golden Arrow" on 15th May 1952. The two civil engineer's sidings are on the right and Abbotts Cliff is in the background. The signal is Folkestone Junction up distant. (J.J. Smith)

93. Abbotscliff signal box was a block post controlling one siding and was photographed on 30th April 1961, ten months before its closure. The Abbotscliff Tunnel, which is 1 mile 182 yards long, commences in the distance. (J.J. Smith)

94. The siding was about a mile east of the two seen near Warren Halt and was marked on the control diagram as Colliery Siding, although the colliery was beyond Shakespeare Tunnel. The box was fitted with standard SR three position block instruments. The 1915 landslip took the signal box with it, the signalman having made a rapid departure to the top of the moving cliffs where he found cracks in the road and a mobile house, which descended 100 ft. intact! (J.J. Smith)

SHAKESPEARE HALT

95. The SER obtained Parliamentary approval for the construction of the Channel Tunnel in 1881. From a shaft 160ft. deep, a 7ft. diameter tunnel, 1¼ miles long, was driven under the sea. On the French side, 1½ miles was completed when the War Office ordered suspension of work. During the sinking of the shaft, coal was discovered which led to the development of the Kent Coalfield. The headgear of two shafts can be seen in the centre of the picture and Shakespeare signal box is in the right background. (British Rail)

The 1907 edition shows the track layout at the Dover Colliery, as the tunnel works had become known. Coal output proved to be disappointing.

SOUTHERN RAILWAY.
This ticket is issued subject to the By-laws, Regulations and Conditions stated in the Company's Time Tables, Bills and Notices. Available on DAY of Issue ONLY.

Ashford (Kent) to

Ashford (Kent)   Ashford (Kent)
Dover Priory   Dover Priory
DOVER   PRIORY

THIRD CLASS   THIRD CLASS
Fare 2/9   Fare 2/9

1169

SOUTHERN RAILWAY.
This ticket is not transferable and is issued subject to the Company's Bye-laws, Regulations and Conditions in their Time Tables, Notices and Book of Regulations.

Folkestone Warren Halt to

Folkestone Warren Halt   Folkestone Warren Halt
Folkestone Jc.   Folkestone Jc.
FOLKESTONE JUNCTION

THIRD CLASS   THIRD CLASS
Fare 2½d.   Fare 2½d.

9369

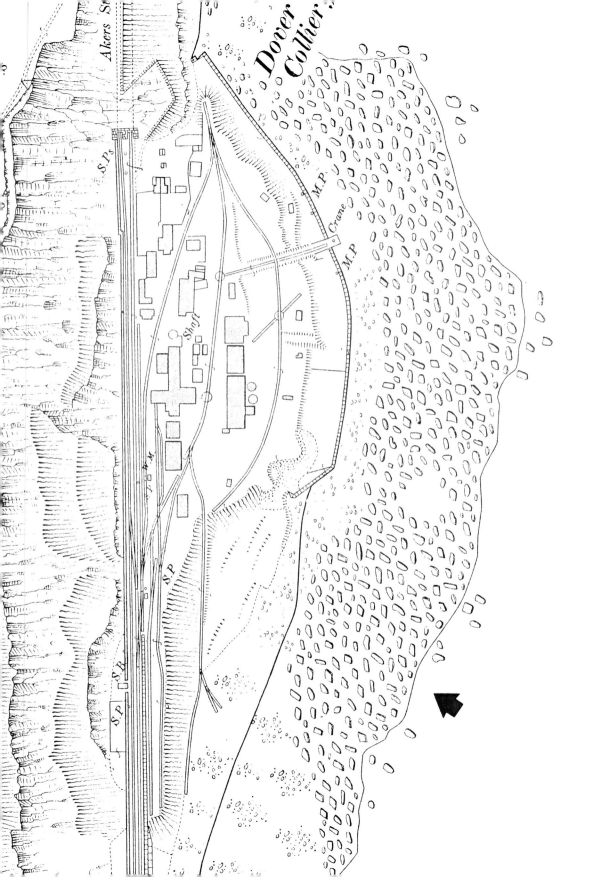

Dover Collier:

Akers S.

S.P.s

M.P

Crane

M.P

Shaft

W.M

S.P

S.P

S.B

S.P

96. Schools class 4–4–0 no. 30924 *Hailey-bury* speeds past the colliery site, with the 9.50 am Charing Cross to Deal service on 30th June 1960. During the construction of the line, Round Down Cliff was blasted into the sea to avoid the construction of a fifth tunnel on the coast. 18,000 lbs. of gunpowder were electrically detonated – advanced technology for 1843. (J.J. Smith)

97. The halt has not been open to the public but, as at The Warren, is retained for staff use together with sidings controlled by ground frames. The former colliery cottages were still standing in 1960, close to the gothic portals of the ¾ mile long Shakespeare Tunnel. Akers Steps are on the cliff face. (J.J. Smith)

98. Repeatedly discussed in Parliament for nearly a century, approval for the Channel Tunnel was given by Mr. Heath's Government only to be cancelled later by Harold Wilson. In the meantime a road tunnel (on the right) was driven from the cliff top and an inclined approach (behind the security caravan) was dug down to the submarine tunnel. This is the deserted scene in 1976, after ½ mile of tunnel had been built. (British Rail)

99. On 20th January 1986, the British and French Governments authorised construction, using private finance. On 1st September, Eurotunnel moved onto the site of the previous attempts and soon Hunslet rack and pinion locomotives were working on the 1 in 7 ¼ mile long access tunnel. BR's first contract was to carry 7000 tonnes of sheet piling from Scunthorpe to the site. The 60ft. lengths are being used to create a pallisade in the sea, behind which 3 million tons of spoil from the tunnel will be dumped. At the time of writing, in January 1988, the rail traffic envisaged over the following three years includes 1,700,000 tonnes of concrete lining segments from the Isle of Grain; 74,000 tonnes of cast iron segments; 870,000 tonnes of aggregates and rock plus 20,000 tonnes of steel piles. (R. Wills)

100. Schools class no. 919 *Harrow* is about to enter the Dover end of Shakespeare Tunnel in 1934. Until 1928, the track in this vicinity was carried above the beach on a timber trestle. While the lines were closed following the Warren landslip in WWII, the tunnel was used for the storage of ammunition trains. (Dr. I.C. Allen)

101. A crew route learning special passes the same location as the previous picture, on 4th February 1961. BR class 4 2–6–4T no. 80137 propels ex-LSWR inspection saloon no. DS1 under the overhead conductor, which was provided to enable the class E5000 locomotives to enter the marshalling yard. (S.C. Nash)

102. Ten MLVs (Motor Luggage Vans) were built to work with EMU boat trains and are normally seen at the London end of such trains. Their collector shoes can be retracted when working over non-electrified lines, using their own battery power. Nos. 68005 and 68001, now class 419, haul an LCGB/SEG railtour, on 15th March 1986, past the freight sidings which often contain unusual vehicles themselves, although from foreign sources. (S.C. Nash)

DOVER TOWN

This 1862 map shows the 1844 SER and 1861 LCDR termini. The Admiralty Pier begins in the bottom right hand corner of the map, SER trains running onto it from 1861 and LCDR services following in August 1864. Two separate platforms, end to end, were built on the pier for the competing companies. A joint line of double track was opened on 15th June 1881 to link the two systems directly and allow the SER direct access to the joint line to Deal. It ran south from the LCDR station, involving the demolition of many dwellings in Round Tower Lane and Round Tower Street, to join the SER between its "Engine House" and Town station. An additional locomotive shed is located west of the turntable, at the foot of the cliffs. The Town station was closed in 1914 and the Harbour followed in 1927. Platforms were provided on the joint line but were removed in 1903.

103. This is the Beach Street facade of the SER Town station. Opened on 2nd February 1844, it remained in use until 14th October 1914, when the SECR concentrated local passenger services at the Priory station. Behind the Guy bus in this 1951 photograph is the former Lord Warden Hotel, but its fine marble porch pillars are just out of view. (Prof. H.P. White)

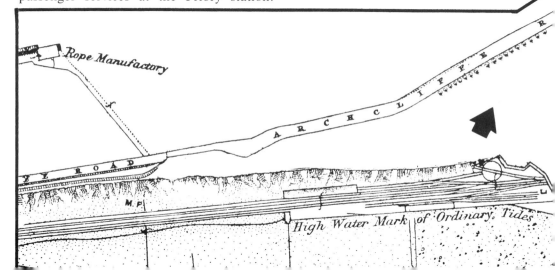

104. Looking west along the main platform of Town station in 1921, we see the twin bores of Archcliffe Tunnel. These disappeared in 1928 when the entire hill was removed, the fort that stood on it having become obsolete. Left of centre is the goods shed, the right hand part of the roof having earlier been continuous with the overall roof of the station – see map. (Pamlin Prints)

105. Turning east, again in 1921, the end wall on the left has a sloping line on it, as evidence of the height of the earlier, overall roof. The down line to the pier curves away on the right, the pedestrian entrance to the Marine station projecting above the vans. The platform on the left remained in use for military purposes until after WWII. (S.C. Nash collection)

106. The former SER engine shed is seen in about 1905, with the lines diverging to Priory and Marine stations in the foreground. The cliff on the left marks the boundary of Archcliffe Fort. After the shed was demolished, eight sidings were laid down and named after the nearby Bulwark Street. (Lens of Sutton)

107. Locomotive facilities were modernised in 1928 by the erection of this shed which had five roads, only one of which ran out at the west end to connect with the marshalling yard. It was built on reclaimed foreshore, adjacent to the site of Archcliffe Tunnel. Owing to the regular German shelling of Dover from guns in France, the depot was only used for coaling purposes during much of WWII. A look-out man was posted to watch for flashes on the French coast – exactly 53 seconds was then available for all staff to take to the shelters. Incidentally, up to 14,000 of the remaining Dover residents slept in the caves at this time. (T. Butcher)

108. The 1928 Archcliffe Junction signal box still remains in use and stands on the end of the former terminal platform (later known as "military platform"), the siding still only being accessible from the up line. Its starting signal is seen in front of the box in this picture of Britannia class 4–6–2 no. 70014 *Iron Duke* leaving with the 6.10pm boat train to Victoria, on 16th May 1952. On the left is the line to Dover Priory and on the right is the locomotive shed, which closed in 1961. (J.J. Smith)

184
KENT & EAST SUSSEX Ry.
CHEAP DAY
Available as advertised.
Dover Marine to
TENTERDEN
Via (S.Ry.) and Headcorn
Third Class
FOR CONDITIONS
SEE BACK
- - - - - - - - - - - - - -
KENT & EAST SUSSEX Ry.
CHEAP DAY
Available as advertised.
Tenterden
Dover M.
Tenterden to
DOVER MARINE
Via Headcorn and (S.Ry.)
Third Class
184

SOUTHERN RAILWAY.
Available for Six Months including Day of issue
Issued only when a MotorCar reservation
has been effected on CARGO BOAT.
Available for ONE SINGLE journey in
either direction between
BOULOGNE & FOLKESTONE HAR.
Third Class.   Fare 12/6
FOR CONDITIONS SEE BACK.
8575   8575

SOUTHERN RAILWAY.
This ticket is issued subject to the Company's
Bye-laws, Regulations & Conditions in their
Time Tables, Notices and Book of Regulations.
London to
DOVER
EXCESS TICKET
Issued in exchange for Third Class
Boat Express Single Ticket to Second Class
(Issued at Victoria)
Second Class.   Fare 8/2
0000   0000

DOVER WESTERN DOCKS

109. The terminus was known as Dover Marine until 14th May 1979, by which time the Eastern Docks had been substantially expanded for handling motor vehicles. This Edwardian view of the Admiralty Pier shows the excellent protection that the wall gave from westerly gales to the platforms. The beach scene on the right is little changed today. The gantry in the distance carried a lighthouse, the assembly being moved seawards as the pier was extended.
(D. Cullum collection)

110. A 1900 post card shows the additional locomotive shed at the foot of the cliffs on the left and the promenade on top of the sea wall of the pier. The area occupied by the two ferries on the right was infilled with chalk just prior to WWI to make space for the construction of the station seen in the following photographs. (Lens of Sutton)

111. A profusion of porters line up as a boat train arrives behind E class 4–4–0 no. 514 in March 1910. The Lord Warden Hotel appears in many views of this area. It was completed in 1851 and for many years had a bridge connecting it with the Town station. A notable resident, until his death in 1931, was Lt.Col. H.F. Stephens, noted for his diverse collection of light railways. Since WWII it has been used as offices, currently by Sealink. (Pamlin Prints)

112. The new station was hurriedly completed at the outbreak of WWI and was not used by the public until January 1919. On the right are the two original lines on the pier and the roof over the staircase that link the high level covered walkways with street level. (Lens of Sutton)

113. The multi-vaulted roof has changed little since photographed in 1921 and all four platforms remain in use today. They are still numbered 3 to 6 although nos.1 and 2 roads on the quayside are no longer in use. A horse makes an unexpected appearance in this exclusively passenger station. (P. Rutherford)

114. An additional platform was provided over ½ mile from the shore, it being approached via Turret Junction which was located close to the bend in the pier. It is here that a new train ferry terminal was under construction in early 1988, having two tracks on the link span and four on the west side of the station. Earlier, steam hauled coaches had been berthed here in some nine parallel sidings, four of which were covered.
(Pamlin Prints)

115. Class B no. 455 pilots class E no. 497 and passes in front of the 1911 signal box. Points of interest in this 1921 view are the unusual boxes over the point rodding and the masonry connection between the Lord Warden Hotel and the station entrance.
(P. Rutherford)

116. The signal box is now separated from the railway it controls by a roadway and the turntable site is now occupied by a customs shed. A 65ft. turntable was provided at the east end of the new locomotive shed. The photograph probably dates from about 1930. (D. Cullum collection)

117. This October 1938 picture shows that key railway installations were protected against bomb and shell blast nearly twelve months before the start of WWII. Dover was named "Hell Fire Corner" during the war – its unique story commands a complete chapter in *War on the Line*, the official history of the SR in wartime, reprinted by Middleton Press in 1984. (British Rail)

118. The up "Golden Arrow" boat train is seen departing on the Folkestone line in 1960, the last complete year in which the train was steam hauled. Conductor rails had arrived in the previous year, when London services via Canterbury had been electrified. The footbridge on the left was also erected then, to give access to the train ferry berth. (Prof. H.P. White)

119. This is one of 24 electric locomotives provided for the Kent electrification schemes. They were also used on freight services and were fitted with pantographs for use in some sidings. E5013 is seen standing under the footbridge prior to departure for Victoria on 30th September 1972, the last day of operation of the "Golden Arrow", famed since its introduction in 1929 for the ultimate in comfort and excellence of table service. (S.C. Nash)

120. London Underground operated an enthusiasts' special on 21st September 1985, using their 1922 ex-Metropolitan Railway electric locomotive *Sarah Siddons*. It is seen here returning from the pier, bound for Clapham Junction via Blackfriars. The tracks beyond the foot crossing were subsequently taken out of use, thus removing run-round facilities. The coaches of arriving trains are now removed by the station pilot, in order to release the locomotive. Despite removal of some sidings, Dover remains an interesting and busy rail centre with a new tidal train ferry berth under construction, south of the passenger terminus. The parts of the local railway system of LCDR origin will be included in a future album. (S.C. Nash)

MP Middleton Press

Easebourne Lane, Midhurst, West Sussex, GU29 9AZ
☎ Midhurst (073 081) 3169

BRANCH LINES
BRANCH LINES TO MIDHURST
BRANCH LINES TO HORSHAM
BRANCH LINES TO EAST GRINSTEAD
BRANCH LINES TO ALTON
BRANCH LINE TO HAYLING
BRANCH LINE TO SOUTHWOLD
BRANCH LINE TO TENTERDEN
BRANCH LINES TO NEWPORT
BRANCH LINES TO TUNBRIDGE WELLS
BRANCH LINE TO SWANAGE
BRANCH LINES AROUND GOSPORT
BRANCH LINES TO LONGMOOR
BRANCH LINES TO LYME REGIS
BRANCH LINES **AROUND** MIDHURST

SOUTH COAST RAILWAYS
BRIGHTON TO WORTHING
WORTHING TO CHICHESTER
CHICHESTER TO PORTSMOUTH
BRIGHTON TO EASTBOURNE
RYDE TO VENTNOR
EASTBOURNE TO HASTINGS
PORTSMOUTH TO SOUTHAMPTON
HASTINGS TO ASHFORD*
SOUTHAMPTON TO BOURNEMOUTH

COUNTRY RAILWAY ROUTES
BOURNEMOUTH TO EVERCREECH JUNCTION
READING TO GUILDFORD

SOUTHERN MAIN LINES
WOKING TO PORTSMOUTH
HAYWARDS HEATH TO SEAFORD
EPSOM TO HORSHAM
CRAWLEY TO LITTLEHAMPTON
THREE BRIDGES TO BRIGHTON
WATERLOO TO WOKING
VICTORIA TO EAST CROYDON
TONBRIDGE TO HASTINGS

STEAMING THROUGH
STEAMING THROUGH KENT
STEAMING THROUGH EAST HANTS
STEAMING THROUGH EAST SUSSEX
STEAMING THROUGH SURREY
STEAMING THROUGH WEST SUSSEX

OTHER RAILWAY BOOKS
WAR ON THE LINE
(Reprint of the SR history in World War II)
GARRAWAY FATHER AND SON
(Biography - includes LNER, Talyllyn and Festiniog Railways)

OTHER BOOKS
MIDHURST TOWN – THEN & NOW
EAST GRINSTEAD – THEN & NOW
THE MILITARY DEFENCE OF WEST SUSSEX
WEST SUSSEX WATERWAYS
SURREY WATERWAYS
BATTLE OVER PORTSMOUTH
A City at war in 1940
SUSSEX POLICE FORCES

*Video also available. Details from
M.P. Videos, 11 Park Crescent, Midhurst,
West Sussex GU29 9ED.